A RELATIONSHIP WITH TRUTH

Poem and Verse

Born in the Canadian Oil Patch

BY

NADEN PARKIN

Cover Design: Diane Feught

ISBN: 978-0-9921640-0-3

Library and Archives Canada CIP data available upon request.

www.nadenparkin.com

I've been blessed.

Not with outstanding athleticism

Not with a lucky lottery

Not with a huge inheritance.

I've been blessed

With hard work

Big mistakes

And deep love.

I dedicate this work to my blessings.

Naden

Contents

Introduction

As I travel around Western Canada in my half ton, driving from province to province, town to town and rig to rig, I find my mind begins to write. Never on paper, always in my head, poems and songs and thoughts of love seem to self-create themselves within me.

A Relationship with Truth is the outcome of years of working and travelling around Western Canada, the pains I have felt, the love I have experienced and the wisdom I have gained.

LISTEN

Listen.

To me

To the things I see

Listen.

Because you believe

And you see what I see

Listen.

To me.

Wake Up

I wake up as my mom walks in,

She says "Naden, it's the AM."

I take a big sniff, and it's toast, eggs and bacon,

Slip out of bed and into the kitchen,

Drip… Drip… Drip…From the coffee,

My dad will soon be sipping,

Just then my little sister whips in,

Innocence, pigtails, she's cute as a kitten,

My bro, he's sitting there flipping

Through his hockey card collection,

If I could've been anything, I would've been just him

Look at my folks and they joke like old friends

Mom says, "Done" and the oven opens

Fresh bread, to soak the yolk in

If you'd asked me then, if this would end,

I'd say, "Nope, no chance."

Then I wake up, as my mom walks in

She says, "Naden, it's the AM."

I take a big sniff, and I smell cow shit

She's been up since dawn and she's exhausted,

4

The farm's costing, so dad had to go,

Chase big oil to send coins home,

"What's going on?" my sister joins in

Still innocent, but with French braids then,

In a bit, my bro fades in

He's grounded, busted drunk with town kids,

"Now kids, your dad sends a kiss

He'd call but, cell phones don't exist."

Just then, the fridge opens

Skimmed milk, cold cereal for breakfast,

If you'd asked me then, if this would end,

I'd say, "Nope, no chance."

Then I wake up, as my dad walks in

He says, "Naden, it's the AM."

I take a big sniff, but my nose is plugged stiff,

Late last night I was stoned with my friends.

No breakfast because dad needs a hand,

Where's mom? She's gone with her new man,

Two families, broke from this one

No innocence left, my sister's with mom.

No fun, and my bro just flew,

Overseas, our home's down to two,

"Just me and you," my dad used to say,

Strong, proud, with tears down his face,

Disgraced, in his home town,

And trust me, that shit flows down

If you ask me now, how I felt back then,

I say, "Nope, no thanks."

Then I wake up, and my mom walks in,

She says "Naden, it's the AM."

I take a big sniff, and its eggs, toast and bacon,

Drift out of bed and into the kitchen,

Drip... Drip... Drip... From the coffee,

My dad will soon be sipping,

Just then my little sister skids in,

Innocence, pigtails, she's cute as a kitten,

My bro, he's grinning there flipping

Through his hockey card collection,

If I could be anything, I would be just him

Adore my folks as they joke like old friends

But then, the dream ends,

I wake up, as Love walks in

She says, "Naden, it's the AM."

I take a big sniff, and its toast, eggs and bacon.

This is coming from Canada.

I'm a,

Midwestern peasant a man of the,

God blessed rednecks with oil patch blood,

Saskatchewan born, now working Albertan muds.

Art is love in its truest form.

Something Inside

Something's in me, living inside,

It's vivid alive,

Just picture my eyes as windows outside

To a kid who's willing to die, for...

3, 2, 1... What shivers your spine?

Visions of mine,

A whole civilization blind, and victimized

As we lie below an invisible line

Beneath, the richest guys

Who bitch and cry over misplaced dimes

While we,

Risk our lives just to wish of times of bliss and pride

To see,

Retired at 65. Is it worth it? To work to die?

No please, don't believe those lies,

Slaves of our time

As am I.

     Something's in me, in me, in me

     It's freaking me out, it's beating me down,

     Eating me up and making me shout

     Something's, making me shout it's, eating me up,

Beating me down and freaking me out

Something, in me.

And it's haunting me, taunting me

Constantly, wanting free, for me to

Break the bonds of slavery, and maybe, that'll take more than bravery,

Because cave ins like shale seams, wake my day dreams

And that reminds me of the mainstreams of my makings

That make their way, to the United States

And that makes me want to shake things

Like rattle the cages of fellow Canadians

Battle like mages while rattling off pages,

Of engravings made by Naden,

I'll saddle up painted, and wage war for the slaves,

Until I'm ancient

Not just Africans, Asians or Canadians,

I'm speaking to the working class Homo sapiens

Because something's in me, in me, in me

It's freaking me out, it's beating me down,

Eating me up and making me shout

Something's, making me shout it's, eating me up,

Beating me down and freaking me out

Something, in me.

Northern Man

I'm the Northern Poet, just a Northern man

Northwest North America's my Northern land

From the west coast to the frozen spans

Of Estevan, then Edmonton

The Alaska Highway and the Pine Pass

Past the Chilcotin flats to West of Van

Then Calgary to Grande Prairie

You ask me, I'd invest in that

It's natural gas and the oil patch

Western Canada, we're blessed with that

And cursed with that

And if you think not, then you're immersed in facts

I'm drunk.

Hammered in fact, stumbling, stammering someone balance me back.

Up.

Love Like Bricks

I met a queen, a queen who won't wear a crown, with such
beauty

Caught somewhere between, a celebrity and a goddess in gown,
more amusing

Than a dream, a dream where I'm lost in the clouds, or a shoot-
ing

Star beam, that's why I'm saying these thoughts out loud, it's a
true thing

And I'll sing loud and I'll sing clear

I'll sing so everyone can hear

That I don't care what anybody says, I'll sing it to the end

That I love you

And I don't care what anybody thinks, that love is made of bricks

And she loves me

I met a girl, a girl who told me her name was Ciana

We saw the world, we took a journey we travelled by plane, to a
land of

Sweat and sunburns, met different cultures yet came from the
same, from Canada

Our stories turned, but pages ended up on the same, so I sang
out

And I sang loud and I sang clear

I sang so everyone could hear

That I don't care what anybody says, I'll sing it to the end

That I love you

And I don't care what anybody thinks, that love is made of bricks

And she loves me too

Dying Inside

I'm dying inside

I've felt the lies

Of a thousand wives

Behind, two thousand eyes

Three thousand infants cried

The instant those wives

Said goodbye.

Love

It's the simple things that can hurt you the most.

The love of a mother,

The friendship of a brother,

The tenderness of a little sister.

What you see, creeps in and makes you feel.

Deceit, distance, disappointment.

I distance myself deep away

Love blinds my expectations

I deceive myself and trust love

Bring love close, and feel everything,

But beware, lose it, and feel even more.

It's a simple thing, that's hurt me the most.

A flat land with a painted sky

Graced by the great herds

But all the grazers died.

Love Can Kill Ya

Let me tell you about terrible dreams of terrible scenes,

Unbearable screams, tearing at her hair and the sheets

Embarrassed I cared, but it's a dream,

But some dreams manifest, so this is real!

Now inside, I'm blazing like Carrie,

Crazy in my cage, I'm barely ordinary

A very imperative event from my youth,

Made me need a veterinary or I'm fleeing the coop,

Not a chicken or a bitch, but I can play Snoopy,

So tell me who, who the fuck you been doing?

You know I've been brewing so you know I'll be cruel,

And you just crossed the line so I'm tearing at you

While staring at you my lip starts to drool,

A werewolf inside and you're my full moon

Too smart too late, too old too soon,

My brain's 15, my heart's 22.

> Because love can ill ya, and love can kill ya,

> And if ya don't know, then let me tell ya

That love can ill ya and love can kill ya,

Blood spills are minimal to victims of oblivia

It's not trivia it's literal, it's been visual,

Since the original days of biblical

Medical and clinical can't explain to this individual's brain,

What's going on when my love turns critical,

I stop thinking, instinct kicks in,

I stop blinking and sweat breaks my skin

I feel deep within, beneath my skin,

And once I'm out I fall back in again

Again and again, when's this shit gonna end?

For infinity, I'm hooked at the hand,

Tick tock tick tock, until the clock ends,

And forget what's said about just being friends

If she don't spread, then he goes and treads,

But he wants her to spread because he doesn't want it to end.

    Because love can ill ya, and love can kill ya,

    And if ya don't know, then let me tell ya

It's a sad fact, but that's how it be,

Happiness of other halves in percent, perhaps 33

I know it's sappy to speak of events that happened to me,

But believe these facts I've seen

Love axe down, my own family tree...

Down on my knees thinking profanities,

Tilt my head back and, "WHAT THE FUCK!" I scream,

At the top of my lungs out at the galaxies,

This disease has taken from me, shamelessly,

And then blameless leaves me,

Tainted, jaded, hatred painted,

In through my veins and arteries

Now constant train hits, monsters in my basement,

I've nailed them in...

But daily maintenance with subliminal brain hints haunt my cranium,

For all eternity.

Because love can ill ya, and love can kill ya,

And if ya don't know, then let me tell ya

The Pit

A victim filled limitless abyss,

I tripped in it, but luckily I gripped the lip,

But my fingertip slipped and my flexor ripped,

Into the pit I fell for infinite minutes,

To the crypts of hell as I yelled, "Forgiveness!"

Into a river, of liquid crimson,

Through slivers of vision I witnessed insects in the distance,

Existing, amongst hordes of demonic minions.

Then a whisper as vivid and crisp as winter

Entered my inner wits with a message delivered

It said, "You better end this, you're better than this, you better get up, before they sever you headless!"

I crept to the edge as insects headed in

I pulled myself free, from that river of death

With my flexor that's wrecked,

I protected my neck and extended my fist with the force of engines of jets

With dissecting effects, all exoskeletons were X'ed out

I turned my attention to my entrance, my best out

Out of breath, I reached for the stone, ignored broken bones, as the demons approached

I leaped toward home and after fifty feet gone

Sweet heat filled my soul, as my heart turned to gold!

"Just keep going!" I screamed all alone

I soared up that hole, leaving the demons below...

It took me ten years, I was fifteen years old,

Now the man you see here,

He's whole.

Mortal's Globe

You'll never know whether I'm clever or slow

I sever with quotes, where weather blows snow

It goes to 40 below and has bears roaming bold

Silhouetted by the setting glow

I'm betting on grow,

Invest my cheque to get some more

A chest of bones protects a heart of gold,

I was blessed born, on this mortal's globe.

A Place Within

I'm alive

I look up at the skies

I see the stars shining on me and it's divine

So I, sacrifice my life to live and rhyme

And shine energies, unlimited supplies.

But it's time to face the times, I'll paint a plain picture

Around flames as rain sprinkles Naden whispers

I'm afraid this is the only way to say my wits

I pray it hits, and I pray it sticks.

As I navigate through this maze of shit

I found a place in Naden where no fake emits

No pain exists, and this amazes him

Now I say to your face find your place within

It's always existed, can bring up waves of sick

But trade that agony and blasphemy for an angels kiss

Tragedy and catastrophe, for angel bliss

Because exactly what'll make you happy actually lays within.

Fly Like That

Ya, I wanna fly like that,

Wanna get fucked up and get high like that,

Kiss the girls, taste the world and never look back.

Ya, I wanna fly like that,

Wanna get fucked up and get high like that,

Eclipse the spotlight, chase the night life and never look back.

Ya, I wanna fly like that,

Wanna get fucked up and get high like that,

Wanna chase my fears, taste my dreams and never look back.

Ya, I wanna fly like that,

Just fly 'til my wings collapse.

Good-bye

I'm caught in this hard place

Having thoughts that make my heart race

I don't want to talk, we know how tears taste

Don't want your pretty face to turn to a wasted grace,

It's a waste of time

And if you only knew that you could taste mine,

Holding you took a place in my mind

A place in my soul, so no smile when I watch you go,

We've built a life and a home

I've

Seen your cold but I've felt your warm

I

Know you're bold but scared to be alone

But you're not meant as my wife, so babe,

I've got to let you go.

A man makes his own decisions

And faces his own consequences

The Cutest Girl

She was the cutest girl I ever knew,

She was the cutest girl I'd ever do,

She was the cutest girl,

And she was mine.

After Love

I look into her soft smile

She asks me, "Can't you stay a while?"

"No, I really have to go."

"But if you go, I'll be alone."

She moves in slow and touches me,

With her nose, with her left cheek,

I brush the hair from her face,

Our lips, embrace.

I guess… I can stay.

My Stoned Bliss

Deeper and deeper, into the bong

Takes me deeper and deeper, into the smog

Deeper and deeper, into a bog

Deeper and deeper, into a fog

It's a haze for days, but I get my work done

Crazy the ways of this gateway drug

It'll change your brain, not always fun

But the pain goes away when it's in my lungs

And I go deeper and deeper, away from this place

Deeper and deeper, in my own space

Deeper and deeper, behind my own face

Deeper and deeper, away from the grace

It calms my hand and slows time down

Makes me the man, makes me act the clown

Makes me hate, "the man" and hate, "the crown"

And hate myself that I can't put it down

As I go, deeper and deeper, I don't know why

Deeper and deeper, into the sky

Deeper and deeper, into the high

Deeper and deeper, inside

Twelve years since my first hit

Shit, twelve years since my folks split

Twelve years, twelve times and I can't quit

Twelve years high, in my stoned bliss

Me

As darkness falls my shadow disappears,

Just like my friends through years, no one's standing here but me,

With this time of soul reflection

I know I own my mind, I'm my own lieutenant.

My own best friend but my own worst enemy

This identity… my mind has befriended me

But sometimes, even I'm second guessing me

And in time, I know it'll be the end to me,

So I, rhyme… it's my energy

An entity with in me, and it's heavenly

But with these sins in me, I don't know where they're sending
me

So hopefully, inevitability cleanses me.

Why I'm Here

I whisper gently for fists of plenty

I've risked my limbs for fistfuls of twenties

And lived with sin that's been around for centuries…

I've kissed the gypsies while sexing,

I've sniffed the shit thats affecting,

I've hit the spliffs with ribs flexing,

Sipped the mix until I'm wrecked,

Ship wrecking, yet investing,

In thoughts of what's witnessed,

Like the plots, of the wicked

What's been lost, in scripture

When history's written by the richest

And that's why I'm suspicious of politics and television,

I've had visions of horrific

Finishes on the course that we're living

      And that's why I fear

      That that's why I'm here,

      No   please   set   me   free…

      Out.

Out to

Chant and torment

In this enchanted forest

Plants and foliage

Turned trash and toilets,

That's massive spoilage,

At home on this globe with the vast annoyance

Of fast deployment of, employment,

What for, some cash and coinage?

What for, some gold that you want to hold

Yet you can't go with?

So I'll keep my full wit,

And my thoughts won't be fooled with

What's shot out that tube, brainwashed to be foolish,

Remain cautious and coolish until I'm rotten and useless,

I'll be gone, I'll be forgotten, but never forget,

What the truth is.

    And that's why I fear

    That that's why I'm here,

    No   please   set   me   free...

    Out.

It's Up to You

Lasers

Shoot out the tube gonna make yer brain hurt

Night vision won't change yer

View of the news gotta use yer main nerve

Or crater

What ya do when ya lose and the music takes yer

Shoes to the moon cause the view is great there

But lose old blue and we're in

Danger

And the way we use crude you can't blame her

Neck through the noose boots down and hang her

See the future's looking screwed

When the few control the huge

And when the few control the fuel

The few control you

It's lose lose unless you choose to

Save her.

I Know

I've got this voice like thunder

Because somebody knows that nobody's under

Control

So I go to the glow until my nose is sunburnt

And spoke 'til my lungs hurt

No, I don't wonder

I know that the snow lasts more than the summer

I know that the cold has the warm at least double outnumbered

I know our folks come from all different sorts

I know it's slow going through the West port

I know that hockey players outnumber our armed force

I know that the force we're North of sort of supports us just
for our resources.

Know that I chose to load this poem with importance

For you to notice.

So pose and ponder

Thought's a choice and I choose to wonder,

For more

So I can grow on my own like I don't need a mother

Like folks are for suckers

Ya, I know who comes first

This world's horny and the poor get fucked first

I know the way we're going we'll end up destroying our one Earth.

I know our folks come from all different sorts

I know that torn are the races by wars

I know that armed forces outnumber our Peace Corps

I know there's a road before us blocked by soldiers and we must march forward

Know that I chose to show this

To let my soul expose what all of you already know

But you hold in.

Oil Patch Poet

Invincible and untouchable,

Every word written becomes indestructible,

God busted the mould when I struck the globe,

Name another oil worker constructing poems.

A Heart of Gold

Two feet on the ground with my eyes wide North

My mind's in the clouds as I'm flying on forth

And I'll, drive on course, so when you find my corpse,

I'll be blind from the shine of the sky courts,

Just a, guy with pride and a drive forward

Never climbed out the slime, I was born with a spine,

So I'm growing wings to soar,

Let heaven hear my heart and let earth hear me roar,

Watch me and I'll defy the norm

I'll hit a spliff and then I'll defy the floor

I'm ripped with sin, but relying on Lord

So when my ribs give in, past the line to the door

And if you'll, miss me then,

Now, you better get more

Life's instant, no time to be bored

No, time to be poor, only time to get more,

So I'll rhyme 'til I find what the fuck, I'm dying for.

      I've got, 2 eyes, 2 balls and 2 feet

      So what the fuck could you have on me,

      Against a heart of gold?

      I've got a heart of gold.

So keep my eyes on the prize and my nose to the grind,

My nose out the blow and my nose out the sky,

Keep my foes in the cold, look my foes in the eye,

Never chose this road, but, suppose I die?

Fuck that, suppose I fly

North road on four three, white rose from Lord kind

Echoes come forth mine, echoes from forced pride,

I'll show you coarse rhyme, I was born to force rhymes,

But unknown to mankind, like a foe of mankind

I'll show you blown minds, open your blind eyes

Open your mind's eye,

To an ocean flowing forth a potion of star shine.

I'm a fortress with one mind..

Reinforced with 2 eyes…

2 balls, 2 feet, and refined,

Transformed, Optimus Prime.

> I've got, 2 eyes, 2 balls and 2 feet
>
> So what the fuck could you have on me,
>
> Against my heart of gold?
>
> I've got a heart of gold.

Hooded Snails

I walk through wooded trails and I talk to hooded snails,

Trains of thought lost, as my thoughts often sail,

I have talked to males, who've tossed out my tales,

So these snails grow in wisdom, as the world stays veiled.

Her Cost

I was born a citizen, a civilian

A working class man, no multimillions,

So I work with that

 I want a Ms. Middleton,

A mansion on a hill where she can dance in silk and,

Watch the stars,

We could

Walk with stars and talk with stars,

We could

Smoke cigars and cough so hard

That we'd fall down

I would hold her heart.

I could kiss her scars

Whisper promises in the blissful dark

My fists would spar

If princess were victim of a singles' charge

From my ribs to my heart

From the furs to the farm to the rigs to the dark

That churns in the earth until it's burned in my thoughts

I can work, until I'm worth,

Her cost.

Groundbirch Camp

As I ride this road my mind stays open

It shows me my soul's older than the host it's chosen

Then from the throat of some old Native woman

She told me she knows me though I know she couldn't

So I stood frozen as cold hands groped my shoulders

And she told me, slowly for moments

"Your old soul glows like it's gold dust,

Expose it, and the whole world will notice."

Use Your Noodle

As my tires turn I see road in my rear view

Past liars, and glass people I see through

A Saskatchewan guy who needs you

But it's cool, just want to teach you

A few things I've learned, outreach to reach you

Deplete fools, think hard and preach true

See our leaders, realize that they're you

Grab your nuts, suck it up and breach through

Keep cool, and abide by these rules

Friends come and go but blood's like pure fuel

Love over money and money over feuds

And when it comes down to it

Be true to you

And choose your path wisely, don't just cruise blindly

Who's behind you when you're driving?

You've got to lose the fools and use your tools

And use your noodle to search for truth,

Instead of just using Google

See Me

See me and see what you see

Beneath the seams it seems he has this need to be seen

But it seems to me that I need to be between

Speaking with people and on my knees to Allohim

So allow me to speak into your dreams

I'm breathing for your needs

Because we need to be freed

So please, turn off your TV

Embrace your neighbors

Believe in human being.

I forgive them, all of them,

They're just trying to be happy,

Everyone's just trying to be happy.

No matter what it is they do,

Everyone's just trying to be happy,

We're all just trying to be happy.

Long Brown Hair

I'm in love

With long brown hair.

I'm in love

With long brown stares.

I'm in love

But she just don't care.

She just sits there, in her chair,

With long   brown   hair.

Start Now

I'm cruising, my hound's riding beside me

I'm moving, the sun's shining on me

I'm choosing, to be a one man army

I'm losing, all that's left behind me

Because it's a free   free   world

And it need   be   circled

Through the cities   through the rural

Hug the trees   grip for pearls

And love   every day that goes by

And love   every hour upright

And love   every minute of life

And love   every second alive

My Prayer for Humanity

Let the clouds part in the sky

Let the sun shine in my eyes

Let the light reflect back to heaven

And Heaven, let every child survive.

Let men share soft emotion

Let women bare soft breasts

Let infants stay soft spoken

And let the dead, rest.

Let TV sets turn down

Let the music be turned up,

Let our nations dance together

Let our kings raise their cups.

To quench

Those who thirst

To feed

Those who starve

To defend

Those who hurt

To mend

Those with scars.

Let my heart, beat strong

'Til my mind dies in my sleep

Let my soul go on forever

And never let my friends weep.

Fight to Survive

As my heart beats in my chest,

I know every second of life can be a test,

So deep breaths of air cold as ice

Because when you're born in the North, that's what it's like.

Like the Northern Lights, we pay a price

Only a few see beauty through the night

There's no Aurora Borealis in the day

Just like our forests won't grow without some rain.

So I thank God when the sky cries,

And I thank God when the sun hides

It's not that I don't hope for blue skies

But we need dark times to appreciate the sun rise.

With no snow, there's no spring,

With no spring, there's no new beginnings,

So when you get low, fight to survive

It's life tests that let us feel alive,

Until we die.

As the Moon Creeps

I was birthed on a small farm,

What gave me worth was that dirt,

But now it's all gone.

Know that it's hurt that keeps me far from,

Scars come from wounds deep as tar sumps.

Now as the moon creeps and stars come

Moon beams lead me to far towns,

To free benzenes, trapped,

Deep down under hard grounds.

That seems easy, when things get busy

And cash comes in large mounds,

But say goodbye to your family, say good bye to your friends

"And get the fuck back to work!" with your head down.

Blue Collar Mayhem

Exaggerations and explanations

From my mouth

My own independent radio station

I've grown to hate this daily race for the paper

Raping nature

Just so my pockets ain't vacant.

Naden's tainted

Can you blame him?

My face stays straight but inside its cave-ins

There's shame in my veins for remaining a layman

So I wake up

Straight for the pay check

Taming natural gas

Propane pays him

Payments to make

What if descendants came in?

So amen

Is what I say when the day ends

God please say when ends meet on minimum wages

Until then

I guess I'm just caged in

My family name has been slaves since days of cave men,

I ache

I just want to break this chain and

Erase the Parkin's day in this blue collar mayhem.

Ancestry

I'm alive

Because this blood in me is pure.

Crude oil reverse 50 years to mink fur

I've survived

Because this love in me is pure.

It comes to me from above this I'm sure

It's inside

It pumps and it churns

Thumps and it burns, a furnace

That comes when I yearn for courage

What I've learned is

Occurrences happen on purpose to persons

Disturbances from perfect and the work hits

Insurance for curveballs as the world twists

Open your eyeballs and observe this

Without life

This earth is worthless

Without rights

Our work is worthless

If I'm right

This verse was worth this

Curtains close on all birthed in sin

When I go

I want to know the world has heard this.

Saskatchewan-kind

I close my eyes and let my mind wander

Back in time to a time when I was younger

Saskatchewan-kind

Half side of me's farmer

Half side's hippy

Inside's artist.

God blessed heart kissed by darkness

A fist of cash

A hippy's conscience

So I call out to God, "Give me strength!"

He responds…

I carry on.

Staring beyond the blank stares of everyone

Shedding love

On anyone.

An ancient love from an ancient place

That originates above.

So I'll brace for rain and I'll face the mud

Wash the shame away as I embrace for floods,

Until the day I break through and face the sun

Just a farm raised hippy

With veins of Naden's blood.

Busy Laying Laminate

Take a look around and see what's going down

What up?

In your city or your town

Shut up!

Listen

 Pity we just clown and get fucked up

When we could be space bound

But

Face down we're slaving and hammering

Maybe lease handing

But

 I ain't having it

Instead of laying with queens

We're laying laminate

Framing cabinets

While a few famous inhabitants

On this blue planet

Fake and make off like bandits

I walk

I feel someone should be walking with me

I talk

I feel someone should be listening

What I See

I wake up

There you are

Half naked

I can see your scars

I can see the stars in your eyes

I see pain

I see your face

I know your name

I stare with love

I stare with awe

You stand close

You seem far

I've seen you smile

 I've seen your tears

I've seen you awhile

Up through the years

I see hope

I see dreams

I've seen the dope

I've seen you fiend

I've seen you come

I can't watch you go

I've seen you with others

Mostly alone

I see you

You see me

Eye to eye

Cheek to cheek

Face to face

Hand to hand

I see me

Man to man

What I Love Doesn't Matter

I love life

I love love

I love peace

I love hugs

I love kisses

I love sex

I love women

I love breasts

I love competition

I love hockey

I love singing

I love talking

I love people

I love the world

I love animals

I love one girl

I love truth

I love knowledge

I love alcohol

So I'm called

Alcoholic.

For Them We Must For Us We Must

I'm a shape shifter

A make shift microphone

As my day shifts to night my excitement grows

I take bliss in the right to cite my quotes

No dang difference

I'd write just to spite my foes

So forthright devout I chose

My inner light outright ignites a chorus

The likes of mighty types of soldiers

Who fight for rights in this life before us

So adore us

We fight like Taurus

More like cobras as we strike the forefront

Born poor grunts

But we try transform us

To royal blood

So they can't destroy us

So join us

Choice appointed

Voice anointed

To the task before us

To pass truths

Bestowed on us

By our forefathers who've

Joined the dust

Truth

Tales and fables

From sharp, double edged sabres

From neighbours and friends

All used as the means to an end

It's the deep end of shallow

For power and for greed

We need to swallow

All that we've chosen to eat

Defeat is not an option

When you're tossed in to the mix

Into an ocean

Where you're shown treats while you're tricked

By critics and liars

Who all climb on each other

While mothers sit and sigh

While their sons try live forever

With hard leather and stone

While bones grow brittle

Withering away a bit each day

Until they just sit and shiver

Quivering

Then die

Then lie

In the earth

Birth light life strife

Box

Dirt

I Knew a Man

I knew a man who was old as the seas

And who knows what he'd seen, through the course of four
seasons

He told me reasons, why I chose believing,

In people he told me… in people, believe.

He said, "Love your neighbour as yourself,

And love your woman, like you love no one else

Love your children, more than yourself

And at the end of two weeks put your boots on the shelf."

He said, "Help your neighbour, if he needs a hand,

And hold your woman, when she needs her man,

Show your children, that they need their dad,

Cause at the end of your life… you'll wish you had."

I knew a man who had never touched clover

Or smelt the roses, he froze every time winter froze over,

With homemade tattoos of his daughter on his shoulder,

He swore, "If I could, I would do it all over."

And he

Loved his neighbour as himself,

And he loved his woman, when he loved no one else

And loved his children, more than himself

And at the end of two weeks ended up by himself

He said, "Help your neighbour kid, if he needs a hand,

And hold your woman close, when she needs her man,

Show your children love, they need their dad,

Cause at the end of your life… you'll wish you had."

I knew a man who had seen what the sky'd seen,

In worn out old boots and with an 'O' imprint in side jean

Holes in his coat sleeves and sorrow where his eyes had been,

With an old sigh, he told me that life means to

"Love your neighbour as yourself,

And love your woman, like you love no one else

And love your children, more than yourself

And at the end of two weeks put your boots on the shelf."

He said, "Help your neighbour, if he needs a hand,

And hold your woman, when she needs her man,

Show your children, that they need their dad,

Cause at the end of your life… you'll wish you had."

My Soulmate

As I push off from the dirt

I've always wondered what I'd find if I left the Earth

Go fly in the sky to the stars

So far that time doesn't exist anymore

Soar past atmosphere and space

Explore with passion and with chase

Past the solar systems and on forever

Discover what's been covered beyond heaven

Where dimensions intertwine

Colors and shapes obliterate my mind

White lines materialize

My body dies and is left behind

My soul keeps going

Until everything's snow white and glowing

Where my heart was

Now is ecstasy

Where I was alone

Now you're next to me

My soul mate

Most days I don't know up from down

But I do know one thing. Keep going forward.

Surviving

When the ground is white and the sky is grey

When the sun shows her face fewer hours in the day

My thoughts turn to nature and it knots my brain

As I play my part to punch holes in her frame

It's for the money

It's for the life

So I can afford the things

I want for my wife

Then the core of me

Turns cold as ice

At the North Pole on a Canadian starless night

It's a hard life when you grow to hate your actions

You pack that weight until your back is cracking

Then you turn and face back stabbing assholes

Who smile

At the same time hope you won't last though

So I just turn North and take a stride

My pace slow

I won't race through this life

I'll face the snow

Below the clouded skies

The Northern Poet

Naden Parkin

Survives

As this page closes I hope you've taken notes

You're a day closer to laying under roses

A shame moments fade as we grow older

So

Feel as what I've shown you and make love before it's over

About the Author

I was born and raised on our family farm outside of Preeceville, Saskatchewan. My father was a farmer and a driller on an oil and gas rig in Northern Alberta and BC. My mother was a stay home mom, who later worked in a hog barn nursery, and is currently working at a dairy farm.

When I was 15 my parents divorced and I went to boarding school at Caronport, Saskatchewan. After high school and a year of college, I headed out under my father's instructions to live with my brother in Camrose, Alberta and began working as a lease hand on a rig near Rimby.

Later, I spent the summer working at a ranch camp and then headed out to another drilling company that I worked with for a year and a half. It was in this time when I first realized that I might like to be a mud man in the oil and gas industry. I later moved to Grande Prairie, Alberta to work and do a few projects with a local musician, and soon after was hired by a company and sent to Houston, Texas to train for a mud man position.

I've continued to live in Grande Prairie, have recently married and continue to work as a mud man in the oil and gas industry, as well as taking the time to create poems and songs reflecting my experiences.

Some things change, some things don't. I still drink whiskey, and I still go to work.

Naden Parkin, Grande Prairie, Alberta, 2014